(Careers in **ARCHAEOLOGY** Part 1)

YOU CAN BE A WOMAN™
EGYPTOLOGIST

Betsy Morrell Bryan
and
Judith Love Cohen

Illustrations:
David A. Katz

Editing: Janice J. Martin

Cascade
Pass, Inc.

www.cascadepass.com

Copyright © 1993 and 1999 by Cascade Pass, Inc.
Published by Cascade Pass, Inc., Suite C-105, 4223 Glencoe Ave.
Marina Del Rey CA 90292-8801
Printed in Hong Kong by South China Printing Co. (1988) Ltd.

Revised Edition 1999
You Can Be a Egyptologist (Careers in Archaeology Part 1) was written by Betsy M. Bryan and Judith Love Cohen, designed and illustrated by David Katz, and edited by Janice Martin.

This book is one of a series that emphasizes the value of science and mathematical studies by depicting real women whose careers provide inspirational role models.

Other books in the series include:
You Can Be A Woman Engineer
You Can Be A Woman Oceanographer
You Can Be A Woman Marine Biologist
You Can Be A Woman Cardiologist
You Can Be A Woman Botanist

You Can Be A Woman Architect
You Can Be A Woman Astronomer
You Can Be A Woman Zoologist
You Can Be A Woman Egyptologist
You Can Be A Woman Paleontologist

Library of Congress Cataloging-in-Publication Data
Bryan, Betsy Morrell.
    You can be a woman Egyptologist/ Betsy Morrell Bryan and Judith Love Cohen ;   illustrations, David A. Katz
          p. cm.
    Summary: The author describes how she decided to become an Egyptologist, what education she needed, and what work opportunities are available in the field of Egyptology.

ISBN 1-880599-45-7 (hbk.)
ISBN 1-880599-10-4 (pbk.)
        1.Egyptology--Vocational guidance--Juvenile literature.   2. Archaeology--Vocational guidance--Juvenile literature. 3. Vocational guidance for women--Juvenile literature. 4. Bryan, Betsy Morrell--Juvenile literature. [1. Egyptology--Vocational guidance.   2. Archaeology--Vocational guidance.   3. Vocational guid-ance. 4. Bryan, Betsy Morrell.] I. Cohen, Judith Love, 1933-   . II. Katz, David A. (David Arthur),   1949- ill.   III. Title.
PJ1085.B79   1999
932' .0072   99-051887

Dedication

This book is dedicated to Elisabeth Bryan whose dedication to her own goals is an inspiration to her mother, Betsy; and to Neil Siegel and Robyn Friend who encouraged their mother, Judith, to learn about the Near and Middle East.

The late afternoon sun has not yet given up its heat, and the breeze gently moves the dust but does not cool. The Egyptian workmen are, of course, at home with this heat, but the young archaeologists do not seem to notice the heat either. Who cares if you're 12,000 miles away from home and haven't seen an ice cube in a month, when any minute you might finally find the foundation of the temple of the rebel king, Akhenaton.

The first few days were terrifying. The future Dr. Bryan didn't miss the conveniences of home nearly as much as the sound and sights of her native language: all those conversations that she couldn't understand, all the street signs and posters that didn't speak to her. But by now she feels at home.

Betsy Bryan is in Egypt for her first "dig," a field trip to dig up an old foundation and find out how the ancient building was laid out. The archaeologists know that there had once been a temple here because several statues had been found years ago; but as yet the building had not been located.

Suddenly, Ahmed, one of the Egyptian workmen, screams out. Is he hurt? Everyone runs to him. Betsy is closest and gets there first. She is stunned by what she sees. There on the ground where Ahmed's shovel has uncovered it, is a piece of an enormous stone head!

The workmen begin to dig around it carefully, and finally the head is uncovered: all three feet of it!

This is not a high-tech, high-budget operation. There is no crane, no lifting equipment. But no matter, because four of the workmen, singing in rhythm with their movements, lift the stone head and carry it to the store house. In fact, that is probably how workmen carried it here in the first place, about three thousand years ago!

Betsy is overwhelmed. This is what she came to Egypt for. This is the dream that has motivated her for fifteen years. How did she get into this wonderful job? Let her tell us her story . . .

It all began when I was ten and growing up in Richmond, Virginia. I read books, loved to swim, played in open spaces, and made up games like cops and robbers.

My favorite aunt gave me a book for my tenth birthday. It was a book about Egypt! I was so taken by the pictures and the story that I told everyone about it. My parents were amused, and although they didn't imagine I would make Egyptology a life-long dream, they were happy to know where to take me for outings and what sort of gifts to buy me. I was often taken to the state museum where I loved to hang out in the room where the mummy was. I also liked all the art objects and artifacts shown there. An artifact is anything made by humans, like coins or dishes or combs.

History was my favorite subject in school. I also liked English literature and science. I especially enjoyed hands-on types of experiments.

Later, I studied languages, especially French. I was already planning my career as an archaeologist, and knew that I would need to be able to read books in other languages, like French.

I always planned to go to college, and my college applications described my dream of "standing in the sands of Egypt doing excavation (digging)."

When I began my studies at the University of Virginia, I majored in European and Asian history and minored in geology and French.

One of my history professors particularly inspired me. I had noticed that many Egyptian statues stood with their left foot forward and seemed to grip something in their right fist. What did their right fist grip? My professor said he didn't know. He went on to tell me that most of the questions I might ask have never been answered. That was good news, because my fear had been that all the work was finished, and there would be nothing left for me to do. But now I knew there was still room for me.

I began by studying Near East languages and literature, and finally specialized in the history and archaeology of ancient Egypt (Egyptology). Archaeology is the study of artifacts as a means of understanding ancient cultures. Egyptology includes archaeology as well as philology (the study of ancient writings).

The Egyptologist begins by thinking about Egyptian culture and some question that he or she would like to know the answer to, like: "What did the Egyptians know about medicine and diseases?"

The next step is to figure out where to look for the answer. For this question, there are probably two directions you can take: you can study about modern medical examination of mummies, or you can study the ancient writings of the Egyptian doctors.

The third step is to actually conduct these studies by examining modern and ancient texts. You might be surprised to find that the ancient doctors performed simple, effective surgery, and that the medications they used did sometimes work. King Tutankhamen (King Tut) was examined and, based on bones and teeth, found to be eighteen years old when he died.

Now that I knew what Egyptology was, I had to learn to do it. Ancient Egypt, the Egypt of the Pharaohs, covers about 3000 years (from 3000 B.C. to the death of Cleopatra in 30 B.C.). Egypt maintained its unique and highly developed culture for the longest time in man's recorded history! For my studies, I chose one specific century to study: from 1400 B.C. to 1300 B.C. King Tut is familiar to many of us, but I was interested in his family: Akhenaten and Queen Nefertiti, Amenhotep III and Queen Tiy, and Thutmose IV.

My first research and book was about Thutmose IV, grandfather of Akhenaten. I wrote the history of his reign and tried to make him more of a real person than a statue.

At the time that these Egyptians lived, the pyramids had already been in existence for over a thousand years. Amenhotep III, Thutmose IV's son, wanted to build new monuments on a scale that no one had ever seen. He wanted to make his capital, Thebes, a center for this new era of art and architecture.

We learned to identify Amenhotep III by his round face and almond eyes. But I wanted to know how thousands of monuments could be made and look so similar, but not be identical. I wanted to study the production of art in all media under this one Egyptian king. How many different artists and workshops were involved, and how could we tell one from another?

Also, pharaohs' names were written inside ovals called "cartouches" to identify their works. I developed a way to study works even if we had no cartouche. Ancient artists drew squares on the walls before they began to paint figures. The squares represented dimensions of the body; for example, 6 squares from foot to knee, 16 to the shoulder, 18 to the hairline. I believed that each artist had his own way of drawing a figure on the squares. Some had long legs, others short, some high waists, others low. I measured hundreds of temple wall figures and statues to find out how many different types there were. And there were only a few. This meant that a few major artists designed the figures.

Other questions I sought answers to involved the roles of women in the years between four thousand and three thousand years ago. Like most people, I already knew about Cleopatra and Nefertiti (King Tut's relative). And like Cleopatra and Nefertiti, the women of ancient Egypt were quite visible. How did men and women relate to one another? What was marriage like?

I decided to look for my answers in ancient Egyptian texts. I found that an Egyptian chief justice had written a book of advice for his son. Later, it was used as a text for school children. And of course, the sculptures and paintings of that era also show relationships between men and women.

What made these texts and this art so interesting is that they showed that love and affection were an important part of marriage in ancient Egypt. Three thousand years later in Europe, this was a very new concept!

Egyptian women could own property, sue people, and work side by side with men. Some women became Pharaoh, and some, like Nefertiti, ruled as co-rulers with their husbands. Also, in tomb paintings I found evidence that a few of the women shown were writers, an indication that women had reached that prized status: literacy!

In order to come to my conclusions, I visited and studied dozens of tombs to capture what they showed in their wall paintings. For example, it was normal for a husband and wife to sit next to one another with their favorite objects under their seats. In some of the paintings, writing instruments were shown beneath seated women. I also translated the Egyptian picture writing (hieroglyphics) on the tomb walls and in various manuscripts written on papyrus (writing material made from a plant).

And remember the mystery that so interested me in college? What were those statues clasping in their hands? Can you believe that I came across the answer a few years later in an article called "An Elusive Shape Within the Fisted Hands of Egyptian Statues"?

The author of this article concluded that the shape was a piece of cloth held much like a handkerchief. Later in Egyptian history, statues held cylinders in the shape of a papyrus roll.

I felt happy about finding an answer to my "clenched fist" question, and with having an example of someone working so hard to find an answer!

BOLT OF CLOTH

How can you tell if you would be a good Egyptologist?

1. Are you interested in traveling to other lands and living with other cultures?

I enjoy the adventure of being in new and different places. After my first surprise at the uniqueness of Egypt, I came to appreciate the kindness, the warmth and the good humor of the Egyptian people. I have always been willing to study and learn other languages and other ways of looking at things.

2. Are you interested in solving problems? Do you enjoy being a detective and following little clues?

I know that I like to solve problems because of the thrill I got from finding evidence that women were literate, and from the joy I feel when I pursue, sometimes for years, the meaning of a picture word.

3. Are you curious about ancient times and peoples? Do you want to know how people lived hundreds or thousands of years ago?

I love history. To read and translate, for the first time in over two thousand years, a letter or a story written by someone who had a family and cared enough about the people in his life to leave a written account, is particularly special to me. In ancient times, writing was as time-consuming as needlepoint is today. There were no electric typewriters or ball-point pens. The ink and the papyrus were expensive and hard to get. The reed pen had to be made by hand, not bought by the dozens at the supermarket. And all of this, before you could even start to write!

What I enjoy most about my career is its variety. For part of the year I'm a teacher. I teach the undergraduate students at Johns Hopkins University about Egyptian culture and history. I also teach the graduate students about ancient Egyptian language, art and archaeology.

During another part of the year I work on a research project, such as the work on Amenhotep III's art. It took many years to collect, exhibit, and catalog this art, and now I am visiting cities here and in Europe with it.

Finally, during the year I might participate in an expedition. I am not mainly a "dirt archaeologist," so my expedition is likely to be to some other museum or perhaps to a site where I will copy temple or tomb wall writing so that I can translate it.

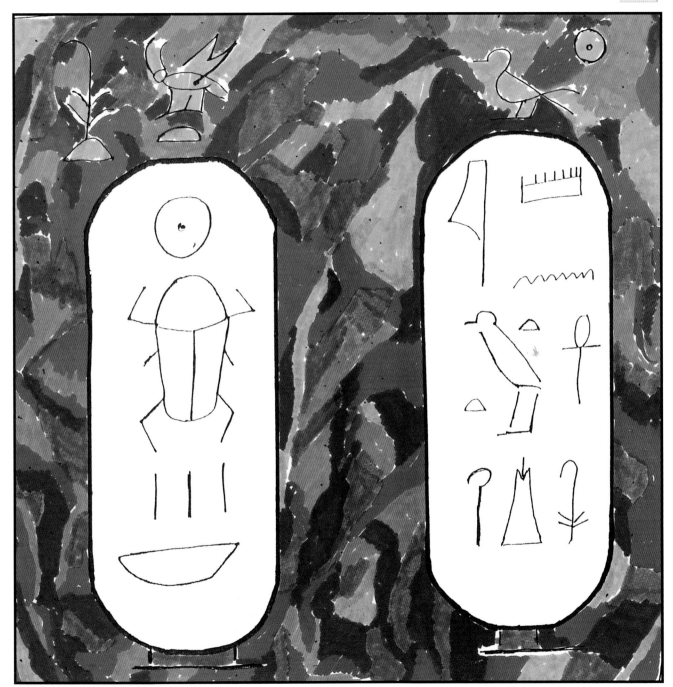

I have two goals in my position as Alexander Badawy Associate Professor of Egyptian Art and Archaeology at Johns Hopkins University.

I would like to do an excavation in Egypt at an 18th Dynasty site (my pharaohs were of that group). I would choose a site that reflected a growing population and changes in land use. And I would like to be involved from start to finish.

I would also like to see my studies in the archaeology of Egypt more connected to studies of other countries. So much writing and art is here for those of us who study ancient Egypt that we often work alone and do not keep up with what is going on in other interesting areas such as Turkey or Greece.

If you want to go to a land where a great civilization flourished, to breathe the very air and walk on the very dirt; if you have to know what really happened from the inside out and learn about people from another millennium (a thousand years); if you want to learn what advice fathers gave to their sons about marriage in the year 1350 B.C. and whether girls went to school in 1000 B.C.; if you are interested in learning to read a language of pictures and knowing what the Egyptians did that kept their civilization going for three thousand years; then you can do it too! You can be a woman Egyptologist.

YOU CAN BE A WOMAN EGYPTOLOGIST

ARCHAEOLOGY LESSON PLAN 1

PURPOSE: To gain an understanding of the processes involved in archaeology.

MATERIALS: Sand, dirt, clay, rocks and gravel.

PROCEDURES: Have children bring in small objects like shells, an old watch, a toy. Have the teacher place the objects in identifiable layers in the sand, dirt, clay or rocks. Have each level stand for a different period of time with the lowest layer being the oldest.

Next, have the children dig the objects out, then draw the objects they find and note the level in which they were found. The children should then clean and categorize the objects.

CONCLUSIONS: What kinds of objects did you find at each level?

What kinds of objects would you expect to find in an ancient Egyptian tomb?

How are your objects and the tomb's objects alike? How are they different?

What would a future generation think about you from studying your objects?

ARCHAEOLOGY LESSON PLAN 2

PURPOSE: To better understand Egyptian art.

MATERIALS: Art supplies (large sheets of paper, crayons, paints, colored pencils, glitter, etc.).

PROCEDURES: Have children write a story on the theme of ancient Egypt. Have the children create a dictionary of picture word symbols (hieroglyphs) that stand for the different words in the story. For example, in Egyptian hieroglyphics, = sun disk symbol.

Have the children draw the story using only picture words, no English words.

CONCLUSIONS: Compare your picture words with Egyptian picture words. Are there any similarities? How are they different?

RESOURCES: Library books on hieroglyphics.

ARCHAEOLOGY LESSON PLAN 3

PURPOSE: To understand the relationship between funeral practices and beliefs.

PROCEDURES: Have the children describe the burial of an Egyptian pharaoh.

Have the children compare this with modern funeral practices.

CONCLUSIONS: What purpose was served by preserving the Egyptian body (mummifying it)? What objects were placed in the tomb? Why? What pictures were on the tomb walls? Why?

How is the modern funeral different?

What does this imply about what we believe today?

RESOURCES: Library books on ancient and modern funeral practices.

About the Authors: Betsy M. Bryan is now the Alexander Badawy Associate Professor of Egyptian Art and Archaeology at Johns Hopkins University. Prior to this, she was a member of the Department of Egyptian Art at the Brooklyn Museum. She received a Ph.D in Egyptology from Yale University in 1980 and has specialized in New Kingdom history and art history. Betsy has studied and cataloged the works of Amenhotep III, king of Egypt, 1290-1350 B.C. She co-curated a traveling exhibition of this work which opened in Cleveland, moved to Fort Worth Texas and is now opening at the Louvre in Paris. Betsy has authored work on both Thutmose IV and his son, Amenhotep III. Her research work has taken her on numerous field trips to Egypt and on trips to museums and libraries around the world.

Judith Love Cohen is a Registered Professional Electrical Engineer with bachelor's and master's degrees in engineering from the University of Southern California and University of California at Los Angeles. She has written plays, screenplays, and newspaper articles in addition to her series of children's books that began with You Can Be a Woman Engineer.

About the Illustrator: David Arthur Katz received his training in art education and holds a master's degree from the University of South Florida. He is a credentialed teacher in the Los Angeles Unified School District. His involvement in the arts has included animation, illustration, and play-, poetry- and song-writing.